Kenya

by Joyce Markovics

Consultant: Marjorie Faulstich Orellana, PhD
Professor of Urban Schooling
University of California, Los Angeles

BEARPORT
PUBLISHING

New York, New York

Credits

Cover, © Andrzej Kubik/Shutterstock and © fstop123/iStock; TOC, © Eric Isselee/Shutterstock; 4, © SerrNovik/iStock; 5T, © EvaRijnkels/iStock; 5B, © Sohadiszno/iStock; 7, © FOTOGRIN/Shutterstock; 8T, © czekma13/iStock; 8B, © Americanspirit/Dreamstime; 9, © Yurasova/Dreamstime; 10, © Sekar B/Shutterstock; 11T, © WLDavies/iStock; 11B, © WLDavies/iStock; 12–13, © Nick Fox/Shutterstock; 13B, © Kiyoshi Takahase Segundo/Alamy; 14, © brittak/iStock; 15, © Vadim Petrakov/Shutterstock; 16, © BSIP/AGE Fotostock; 17, © Bartosz Hadyniak/iStock; 18–19, © Syldavia/iStock; 19B, © EunikaSopotnicka/iStock; 20, © IMPALASTOCK/iStock; 20–21, © John Warburton-Lee Photography/Alamy; 22T, © Emma Kadenyi Ombima/Shutterstock; 22B, © Philippe Lissac/picture-alliance/Godong/Newscom; 23, © Walid Kilonzi/Shutterstock; 24–25, © Ukrphoto/Dreamstime; 25T, © hadynyah/iStock; 26, © Maisant Ludovic/Hemis/Alamy; 27, © Eric Lafforgue/Alamy; 28, © Pierre-Yves Babelon/Shutterstock; 29, © Caters News/ZUMA Press/Newscom; 30T, © Anton_Ivanov/Shutterstock and © Janusz Pienkowski/Shutterstock; 30B, © Joerg Boethling/Alamy; 31 (T to B), © agafapaperiapunta/iStock, © Sung Yee Tchao/Dreamstime, © WLDavies/iStock, © Andrzej Kubik/Shutterstock, and © LukaKikina/Shutterstock; 32, © severjn/Shutterstock.

Publisher: Kenn Goin
Senior Editor: Joyce Tavolacci
Creative Director: Spencer Brinker
Design: Debrah Kaiser
Photo Researcher: Thomas Persano

Library of Congress Cataloging-in-Publication Data

Names: Markovics, Joyce L., author.
Title: Kenya / by Joyce Markovics.
Description: New York, New York : Bearport Publishing, 2019. | Series: Countries we come from | Includes bibliographical references and index.
Identifiers: LCCN 2018044175 (print) | LCCN 2018045129 (ebook) | ISBN 9781642802658 (ebook) | ISBN 9781642801965 (library)
Subjects: LCSH: Kenya—Juvenile literature.
Classification: LCC DT433.522 (ebook) | LCC DT433.522 .M375 2019 (print) | DDC 967.62--dc23
LC record available at https://lccn.loc.gov/2018044175

For more information, write to Bearport Publishing Company, Inc., 45 West 21st Street, Suite 3B, New York, New York 10010. Printed in the United States of America.

10 9 8 7 6 5 4 3 2 1

Contents

This Is Kenya

WILD

Soaring

PROUD

Kenya is a big country in East Africa.

Over 47 million people live there!

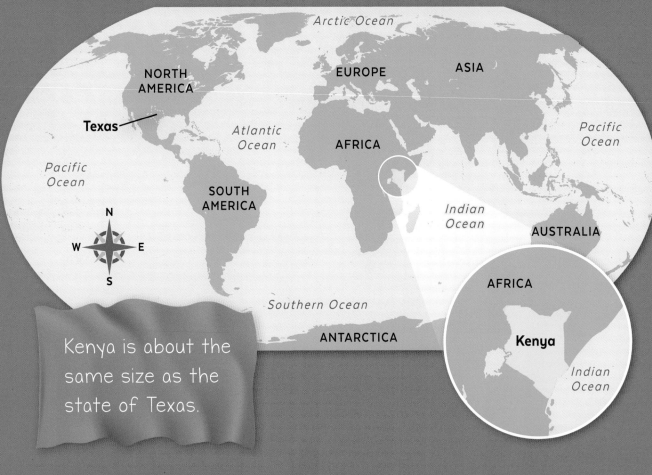

Kenya is about the same size as the state of Texas.

Kenya has every kind of land.

There are **savannas**, mountains, and deserts.

Mount Kenya is the second-tallest mountain in Africa. It used to be a **volcano**!

Mount Kenya

There are big lakes, too.

Lake Victoria

Kenya's Lake Victoria is
the largest lake in Africa!

Kenya is famous for its wildlife.

Huge elephants and giraffes roam the land.

Fierce lions hunt zebras
and wildebeests.

Millions of wildebeests
migrate through
Kenya each year.

Great Rift Valley

A large valley stretches across Kenya.

It's called the Great Rift Valley.

The bones of early humans have been found there.

Some of them date back millions of years!

In 1984, the skeleton of an eight-year-old boy was found in the valley. It's around 1.6 million years old!

The Maasai (mah-SAHY) people live near the Great Rift Valley.

They raise cattle and live in mud homes.

The Maasai are very tall and often wear red robes.

Young Maasai men jump to show off their strength!

More than 60 languages are spoken in Kenya.

The main language is Swahili.

This is how you say *hello* in Swahili:

Hujambo
(hoo-JAM-bow)

This is how you say *friend*:

Rafiki
(rah-FEE-kee)

Many Kenyans learn English in school.

The **capital** of Kenya is Nairobi (nahy-ROH-bee).

It's also the country's largest city.

Over 3 million people live there.

People travel around the city in painted buses. They are called *matatus*.

matatu

Many Kenyans wear *kangas.*

These large cloths are bright and colorful.

Often, kangas have special messages printed on them!

They can be worn around the waist or chest.

Which foods are popular in Kenya?

Ugali (oo-GAH-lee) is made with corn flour and water.

ugali

It's eaten plain or with a tasty stew.

For dessert, Kenyans enjoy fried, sweet dough. It's called *mahamri*.

Many of the world's greatest runners are Kenyan.

Children grow up running.

Some run several miles to school each day!

Soccer is another popular sport in Kenya.

The biggest **festival** in Kenya is the Mombasa Carnival.

People dance in the streets.

During a festival in Lamu, people race donkeys!

Lamu is an island in Kenya. The Lamu festival takes place in November.

27

More than 75,000 people visit Kenya each year.

Most people come to see the wildlife.

At Giraffe Manor, guests can feed a wild giraffe!

A giraffe's tongue can be 20 inches (51 cm) long!

Fast Facts

Capital city: Nairobi

Population of Kenya: Over 47 million

Main languages: Swahili and English

Money: Kenyan shilling

Major religions: Christianity and Islam

Neighboring countries: Ethiopia, Somalia, Sudan, Tanzania, and Uganda

Cool Fact: Much of the world's cut flowers are grown in Kenya!

capital (KAP-uh-tuhl) the city where a country's government is based

festival (FESS-tuh-vuhl) a celebration held at the same time each year

migrate (MYE-grate) to move from one place to another at a certain time of the year

savannas (suh-VAN-uhz) large, open grasslands with few trees

volcano (vol-KAY-noh) an opening in the Earth's surface from which melted rock or ash shoots out

31

Index

Read More

Bartell, Jim. *Kenya (Exploring Countries).* Minnetonka, MN: Bellwether Media (2011).

Burns, Kylie. *Cultural Traditions in Kenya.* New York: Crabtree (2015).

Learn More Online

To learn more about Kenya, visit
www.bearportpublishing.com/CountriesWeComeFrom

FACING MOUNT KENYA
30c
KENYA UHURU 1963

About the Author

Joyce Markovics lives in Ossining, New York.
She has written over 100 books for young readers.
She would like to thank Marilyn Solomon
for her help researching this book.